For Rabbi Justin David:
thank you for sharing the story of Ketzel
L. N.

To my mom, for making me practice
A. J. B.

Text copyright © 2015 by Lesléa Newman
Illustrations copyright © 2015 by Amy June Bates

First edition 2015
This edition published specially for KiwiCo 2022 by Candlewick Press

Library of Congress Catalog Card Number 2013957479

ISBN 978-0-7636-6555-5 (Candlewick trade edition)
ISBN 978-1-5362-2961-5 (KiwiCo edition)

22 APS 1

Printed in Humen, Dongguan, China

This book was typeset in Dante.
The illustrations were done in watercolor, gouache, and pencil.

Candlewick Press
99 Dover Street
Somerville, Massachusetts 02144

www.candlewick.com

KETZEL,
the CAT who COMPOSED

Lesléa Newman

illustrated by Amy June Bates

CANDLEWICK PRESS

MOSHE COTEL LIVED in the middle of a noisy building in the middle of a noisy street in the middle of a noisy city. But Moshe didn't mind. Everything he heard was music to his ears.

Moshe was a composer. Every morning he composed himself by sitting very still. He listened outside himself and listened inside himself, just as his teacher had taught him when he was a little boy. When he was done listening, Moshe turned all the wonderful sounds he heard into beautiful music.

When Moshe was finished
working for the day, he went out for an
afternoon walk to listen to the sounds of the city.
One particular day, he turned a corner and heard
a sound he had never heard on the street before.

It was a small sound.
It was a sad sound.
It was a . . .

"Little *ketzel!*" Moshe cried. He often used Yiddish words when he was nervous or excited. "Come, little Ketzel," he said, scooping up the black-and-white kitten. "I will take you home, and we will make beautiful music together."

The next morning, Moshe moved a stack of music books off the top of the piano and set Ketzel down. "You must listen outside yourself and inside yourself," he instructed as he began to play.

Ketzel kept very still. The music started off softly and slowly. But then it grew louder and faster, reminding Ketzel of crowds of people rushing by her, almost trampling her, and she meowed in fright.

Moshe stopped playing, picked up little Ketzel, and looked into her big green eyes. "Ah, Ketzel, I see that music stirs your soul," he said. "And that is a wonderful thing."

One day, a letter for Moshe arrived in the mail. "The *Paris New Music Review* is having a contest," Moshe read aloud to Ketzel. "Each composition must be no longer than sixty seconds." Moshe blinked in disbelief. "Sixty seconds? Impossible! How can anyone create a beautiful composition in only sixty seconds?" he asked Ketzel, and put the letter aside.

The next day when Moshe sat down to play, his fingers fumbled over the keys. He kept glancing at the letter from the *Paris New Music Review*. Finally, he decided to give it a try. He wrote a few notes, and then a few more, and then a few more. Before he knew it, his composition was ten minutes long. "Impossible," Moshe said.

Time passed, and Moshe grew more and more unhappy. One day he did not even come to the piano at all. Ketzel stared at him as he stared out the window. Ketzel didn't know if he was listening outside himself or listening inside himself. Perhaps he was not listening at all.

Moshe looked at the letter announcing the contest again, and Ketzel looked at it, too. She knew it was the source of all Moshe's unhappiness. Maybe if she got rid of it, Moshe would be happy again.

She put one six-toed paw down on the keyboard, crept across the keys, then pushed off the piano with all four paws and landed on the table where the letter lay.

Moshe whipped around. "Ketzel, that was magnificent!" he cried.
Moshe grabbed a pencil and jotted down exactly what he'd heard.
He played it several times, then turned to Ketzel. "Your composition
has a clear beginning, middle, and end, is full of heart, and takes exactly
twenty-one seconds to play. Ketzel, you're a genius!"

Moshe folded up Ketzel's composition and wrote a note to the judges. "This piano solo, 'Piece for Piano: Four Paws' was written by Ketzel Cotel. It is her first composition. She hopes you enjoy it."

Then he and Ketzel walked to the corner and dropped it in the mail.

Time passed, and Moshe and Ketzel forgot all about the contest.
Then one day another letter arrived.

Dear Ketzel Cotel,

We are sorry to inform you that your
piano solo did not win first, second,
or third place in our competition.
However the judges admired your
creative instinct and imagination and
have decided to award you a certificate
of special mention.

Congratulations!

"Ketzel, you did it!" Moshe cried. He lifted Ketzel in the air, and the
two composers danced a jig of joy all around the room.

A few weeks later, Moshe brushed Ketzel's fur until it shone and put on his very best suit. Then they hailed a taxi and rode to the concert hall where Ketzel's piano solo was having its debut.

Moshe carried Ketzel inside his jacket and sat down in the very last row. When the concert hall darkened, he placed Ketzel on his lap. The music began. Two whole hours went by.

Finally a young girl crossed the stage. "I will now play 'Piece for Piano: Four Paws' by Ketzel—"

"Meow!"

The girl paused, then began again. "I will now play 'Piece for Piano: Four Paws' by Ketzel—"

"Meow!" Ketzel mewled again at the sound of her name.

As the audience laughed, the house manager flicked on the lights and rushed to the stage. "Is there a cat in the hall?" he demanded. "That is not allowed. Please leave immediately."

"But this is Ketzel Cotel, the cat who composed 'Piece for Piano: Four Paws,'" Moshe said, holding up Ketzel for all to see.

"A cat who composes?"

"Ridiculous!"

"Ludicrous!"

"Preposterous!"

"Impossible!"

The judges were called to the stage to confer. "There is no rule saying that a cat cannot compose," the head judge announced. "Therefore, we invite Ketzel"—he paused as she meowed again—"to please stay as we all enjoy her prize-winning composition."

The young pianist took her place. With arms stiff and hands held straight over the keys, she leaned forward, pausing for a minute, like a cat getting ready to pounce. Then she played Ketzel's piece.

"Encore! Encore!" the audience cried.

The girl played Ketzel's composition again, and when she was done,
Moshe brought Ketzel up to the stage so that the composer and musician
could each take a bow.

After the concert, Ketzel became very famous. Her picture appeared in many newspapers, and her composition was performed all over the world. And one day, another envelope addressed to Ketzel Cotel arrived. It contained a royalty payment for nineteen dollars and seventy-two cents.

At the bank, a clerk pulled out a stamp pad, and Ketzel pressed her front paw into the ink and then placed it on the back of the check, endorsing it with her six-toed signature. The bank clerk counted out Ketzel's money.

It bought Ketzel a great deal of cat food, which she thoroughly enjoyed.

AUTHOR'S NOTE

Ketzel, the Cat Who Composed is based on a true story.

Morris Moshe Cotel was born in Baltimore, Maryland, on February 20, 1943. He studied music as a boy, and by the time he was thirteen, he had composed a two-hundred-page four-movement symphony. Mr. Cotel graduated from the Juilliard School of Music in New York City. For many years, he taught music composition at the Peabody Conservatory of Johns Hopkins University.

Ketzel was born in 1992. According to Mr. Cotel, her best-loved composer was Johann Sebastian Bach. On the day that Ketzel strolled down the keyboard, Mr. Cotel quickly wrote down the notes exactly as he heard them. Later, he entered Ketzel's "exquisite atonal miniature" in the *Paris New Music Review* One-Minute Competition, where it received a special mention. In the actual letter sent to Ketzel, the judges praised the composer for her "creative instinct and imagination."

"Piece for Piano: Four Paws" had its world premiere at the Friedberg Concert Hall at the Peabody Conservatory on January 21, 1998. It was played by ten-year-old pianist Shruti Kumar. Ketzel did not attend that performance but did attend a later one and meowed loudly at the sound of her name when her piece was introduced, much to the audience's delight.

Ketzel became quite famous for her piano piece. Mr. Cotel said she was his best student and was amused at how quickly her fame surpassed his own. After her piece was played in Europe, Ketzel received a royalty payment for $19.72, which was used to purchase cat food.

In 1999, Mr. Cotel composed "Mews' Muse for Orchestra," a composition based on Ketzel's prize-winning solo. He retired from teaching in 2000 and was ordained as a rabbi three years later. Speaking to the *Johns Hopkins Gazette* about Ketzel's accomplishment, he said, "The rabbis speak of *kavannah,* a state of mental concentration. Any commonplace event in our day can be transformed and seen in a heightened sense of reality. We are surrounded by miracles if you can only perceive them."

Ketzel's composition can be heard on the CD *Don't Panic! 60 Seconds for Piano.* It is performed by Guy Livingston, the co-founder and editor of the *Paris New Music Review,* who oversaw the contest that awarded Ketzel her certificate of special mention.

Lesléa Newman is the author of more than sixty books for readers of all ages, including *The Best Cat in the World*, illustrated by Ronald Himler, and *Hachiko Waits*, illustrated by Machiyo Kodaira, as well as several other books about dogs and cats. She lives in Holyoke, Massachusetts.

Amy June Bates has illustrated more than forty books for children, including *Waiting for the Magic* by Patricia MacLachlan and *The Dog Who Belonged to No One* by Amy Hest. Amy June Bates lives in Carlisle, Pennsylvania.